The Word

The Most Powerful Word Ever Spoken

The Parables of Jesus

VICTOR BOOKS

A DIVISION OF SCRIPTURE PRESS PUBLICATIONS INC.
USA CANADA ENGLAND

Contents

Preface 3
The Purpose of Parables 4
The Lamp under the Bowl 5
The Wise and Foolish Builders 5
New Cloth on Old Coat 6
New Wine in Old Skins 7
Sower and Soils 8
The Meaning of the Parable 9
The Weeds and the Wheat 10
Matthew 13:36-43 11
Explaining the Parable 11
Mustard Seed 12
Hidden Treasure 12
Yeast 13
The Valuable Pearl 14
The Net 15
The Owner of the House 17
The Lost Sheep 19
The Unmerciful Servant 20
The Vineyard Workers 22
The Two Sons 25
The Tenants 27

The Wedding Banquet 29
The Fig Tree 30
The Faithful and the Wise Servant 31
The Ten Virgins 33
The Talents 34
The Sheep and the Goats 37
The Growing Seed 39
The Watchful Servants 39
The Moneylender 41
The Good Samaritan 43
The Friend in Need 44
The Rich Fool 45
The Unfruitful Fig Tree 47
The Low Seat at the Feast 49
The Great Banquet 51
The Cost of Discipleship 52
The Lost Coin 53
The Prodigal Son 54
The Shrewd Manager 57
The Rich Man and Lazarus 59
The Master and the Servant 61
The Persistent Widow 62
The Pharisee and the Tax Collector 63

THE WORD 4
The Parables of Jesus

Copyright © 1994 by Victor Books/SP Publications, Inc. Original edition published in Denmark under the title, THE WORD, The Parables of Jesus by Scandinavia Publishing House, Copenhagen, Denmark. Copyright © 1993 Scandinavia Publishing House.

Text Copyright © Holy Bible, New International Version®, 1973, 1978, 1984 by International Bible Society. Used by permission of Zondervan Publishing House. All rights reserved.

ISBN: 1-56476-256-4
1 2 3 4 5 6 7 8 9 10 Printing / Year 98 97 96 95 94
Printed in Singapore

Preface

In the beginning was the Word,
and the Word was with God,
and the Word was God.
He [Jesus] was with God in the beginning.
Through him all things were made;
without him nothing was made that has been made.

John 1:1-3

By the word of the Lᴏʀᴅ were the heavens made,
their starry host by the breath of his mouth.
He gathers the waters of the sea into jars;
he puts the deep into storehouses.
Let all the earth fear the Lᴏʀᴅ;
let all the people of the world revere him.
For he spoke, and it came to be;
he commanded, and it stood firm.

Psalm 33:6-9

He is the image of the invisible God,
the firstborn over all creation.
For by him all things were created:
things in heaven and on earth, visible and invisible,
whether thrones or powers or rulers or authorities;
all things were created by him and for him.
He is before all things,
and in him all things hold together.

Colossians 1:15-17

In these last days he has spoken to us by his Son,
whom he appointed heir of all things,
and through whom he made the universe.
The Son is the radiance of God's glory
and the exact representation of his being,
sustaining all things by his powerful word.

Hebrews 1:2-3

3

The Purpose of Parables

Matthew 13:10-17

The disciples came to him and asked,
"Why do you speak to the people in parables?"
He replied,
*The knowledge of the secrets of the kingdom
of heaven has been given to you,
but not to them.
Whoever has will be given more,
and he will have an abundance.
Whoever does not have,
even what he has will be taken from him.
This is why I speak to them in parables:*

*Though seeing,
they do not see; though hearing, they do
not hear or understand.
In them is fulfilled the prophecy of Isaiah:*

**"You will be ever
hearing but never understanding;
you will be ever seeing but
never perceiving.
For this people's
heart has become calloused;
they hardly hear with their ears,
and they have closed their eyes.
Otherwise they might see
with their eyes, hear with their ears,
understand with their hearts and
turn, and I would heal them."**

*But blessed are
your eyes because they see,
and your ears because they hear.
For I tell you the truth,
many prophets and righteous men
longed to see what you see but did not see
it, and to hear what you hear but did not
hear it.*

The Lamp under the Bowl

Matthew 5:14-15

**You are
the light of the world.**
A city on a hill cannot be hidden.
Neither do people light a lamp
and put it under a bowl.
Instead they put it on
its stand, and it gives light to
everyone in the house.

The Wise and Foolish Builders

Matthew 7:24-27

Therefore everyone who hears
these words of mine and puts them
into practice
is like a wise man who built his
house
on the rock.

The rain came down, the streams
rose,
and the winds blew and beat
against that house;
**yet it did not fall, because it had
its foundation on the rock.**

But everyone who hears these
words
of mine and does not put them into
practice
is like a foolish man who
built his house on sand.
The rain came down, the streams
rose, and the winds blew and beat
against that house,
**and it fell with a great
crash.**

5

New Cloth on Old Coat

Matthew 9:14-16

Then John's disciples came and asked him, "How is it that we and the Pharisees fast, but your disciples do not fast?" Jesus answered,

How can the guests of the bridegroom mourn while he is with them?

The time will come when the bridegroom will be taken from them; then they will fast.

No one sews a patch of unshrunk cloth on an old garment, for the patch will pull away from the garment, making the tear worse.

New Wine in Old Skins

Matthew 9:17

Neither do men pour new wine into old wineskins.

If they do, the skins will burst, the wine will run out and the wineskins will be ruined.

No, they pour new wine into new wineskins, and both are preserved.

Sower and Soils

Matthew 13:3-9

Then he told them many things in parables, saying:

A farmer went out to sow his seed. As he was scattering the seed, some fell along the path, and the birds came and ate it up.

Some fell on rocky places, where it did not have much soil. It sprang up quickly, because the soil was shallow. But when the sun came up, the plants were scorched, and they withered because they had no root.

Other seed fell among thorns, which grew up and choked the plants. Still other seed fell on good soil, where it produced a crop— a hundred, sixty or thirty times what was sown.

He who has ears, let him hear.

The Meaning of the Parable

Matthew 13:18-23

*Listen then to what the parable
of the sower means:
When anyone hears the
message about the kingdom and
does not understand it, the evil
one comes and snatches away
what was sown
in his heart.
This is the seed sown along the
path.
The one who received the seed
that fell on rocky places is the
man who hears the word and at
once receives
it with joy.
But since he has no root,
he lasts only a short time. When
trouble or persecution comes
because of the word, he quickly
falls away.
The one
who received the seed
that fell among the thorns is the
man who hears the word,
but the worries of this life
and the deceitfulness of wealth
choke it,
making it unfruitful.*

**But the one who received
the seed that fell on good soil
is the man who hears the word
and understands it.
He produces a crop,
yielding a hundred, sixty or
thirty times what was sown.**

The Weeds and the Wheat

Matthew 13:24-30

Jesus told them another parable:
The kingdom of heaven is like a man who sowed good seed in his field.

But while everyone was sleeping, his enemy came and sowed weeds among the wheat, and went away.
When the wheat sprouted and formed heads, then the weeds also appeared.
The owner's servants came to him and said, "Sir, didn't you sow good seed in your field? Where then did the weeds come from?"
"An enemy did this," he replied.
The servants asked him, "Do you want us to go and pull them up?"

"No," he answered, "because while you are pulling the weeds, you may root up the wheat with them. Let both grow together until the harvest.

"At that time I will tell the harvesters: First collect the weeds and tie them in bundles to be burned; then gather the wheat and bring it into my barn."

Explaining the Parable

Matthew 13:36-43
His disciples came to him and said, "Explain to us the parable of the weeds in the field."
He answered,

*The one who sowed
the good seed is the Son of
Man.
The field is the world,
and the good seed stands for
the sons of the kingdom.
The weeds are the sons
of the evil one, and the enemy
who sows them is the devil.
The harvest is
the end of the age, and the
harvesters are angels.*

*As the weeds are pulled
up and burned in the fire, so it
will be at the end of the age.
The Son of Man
will send out his angels, and
they will
weed out of his kingdom
everything that causes sin and
all who do evil.
They will throw them into
the fiery furnace, where there
will be weeping and gnashing
of teeth.*

**Then the righteous
will shine like the sun in the
kingdom of their Father.**

*He who has ears,
let him hear.*

Mustard Seed

Matthew 13:31-32

He told them another parable: *The kingdom of heaven is like a mustard seed, which a man took and planted in his field. Though it is the smallest of all your seeds, yet when it grows, it is the largest of garden plants and becomes a tree, so that the birds of the air come and perch in its branches.*

Hidden Treasure

Matthew 13:44

The kingdom of heaven is like treasure hidden in a field. When a man found it, he hid it again, and then in his joy went and sold all he had and bought that field.

Yeast

Matthew 13:33

He told them still another parable: *The kingdom of heaven is like yeast that a woman took and mixed into a large amount of flour until it worked all through the dough.*

The Valuable Pearl

Matthew 13:45-46

*Again, the
kingdom of
heaven is like a
merchant looking
for fine pearls.*

*When he found
one of great
value,
he went away
and sold
everything he
had
and bought it.*

The Net

Matthew 13:47-51

Once again, the kingdom of heaven is like a net that was let down into the lake and caught all kinds of fish. When it was full, the fishermen pulled it up on the shore. Then they sat down and collected the good fish in baskets, but threw the bad away.

This is how it will be at the end of the age. The angels will come and separate the wicked from the righteous and throw them into the fiery furnace, where there will be weeping and gnashing of teeth.

Have you understood all these things? Jesus asked. "Yes," they replied.

The Owner of the House

Matthew 13:52

He said to them,
Therefore every
teacher
of the law
who has been
instructed
about the kingdom
of heaven
is like the owner
of a house
who brings out
of his storeroom
new treasures
as well as old.

The Lost Sheep

Luke 15:1-7

Now the tax collectors
and "sinners" were all gathering
around to hear him.
But the Pharisees
and the teachers of the law
muttered,
"This man welcomes sinners and
eats with them,"
Then Jesus told them this parable:

*Suppose one of you
has a hundred sheep and loses
one of them.*

*Does he not leave the ninety-nine
in the open country and go after
the lost sheep
until he finds it?*

*And when he finds it,
he joyfully puts it
on his shoulders
and goes home.*

*Then he calls his friends
and neighbors together and
says,*

*"Rejoice with me; I have found
my lost sheep."*

**I tell you
that in the same way
there will be more rejoicing
in heaven over one sinner
who repents than over
ninety-nine righteous
persons who do not need to
repent.**

The Unmerciful Servant

Matthew 18:21-35

Then Peter came to Jesus
and asked,
"Lord, how many times shall I
forgive my brother when he sins
against me?
Up to seven times?"
Jesus answered,

I tell you,
not seven times,
but seventy-seven times.
Therefore,
the kingdom of heaven
is like a king who wanted to
settle accounts with his
servants.
As he began the settlement,
a man who owed him ten
thousand talents was brought
to him.
Since he was not able to pay,
the master ordered that he
and his wife and his children
and all that he had be sold to
repay the debt.
The servant fell on his knees
before him.
"Be patient with me," he
begged,
"and I will pay back
everything."
The servant's master took pity
on him, canceled the debt and
let him go.
But when that servant went
out,

he found one of his fellow servants who
owed him a hundred denarii.
He grabbed him and began to choke him.
"Pay back what you owe me!" he demanded.
His fellow servant fell to his knees and begged him, "Be patient with me,
and I will pay you back."
But he refused.
Instead, he went off
and had the man thrown into prison
until he could pay the debt.
When the other servants saw what had happened, they were greatly distressed and went and told their master everything that had happened.
Then the master called the servant in.
"You wicked servant," he said, "I canceled
all that debt of yours
because you begged me to.
Shouldn't you have had mercy on your fellow servant just as I had on you?"
In anger his master turned him over to the jailers to be tortured, until he should pay back all he owed.

This is how my heavenly Father will treat each of you unless you forgive your brother from your heart.

The Vineyard Workers

Matthew 19:28–20:16

Jesus said to them,
I tell you the truth,
at the renewal of all things,
when the Son of Man sits on his glorious
throne,
you who have followed me
will also sit on twelve thrones,
judging the twelve tribes of Israel.
And everyone who has left
houses or brothers or sisters or father or
mother or children or fields
for my sake will receive a hundred times
as much and will inherit eternal life.
But many who are first will be last, and
many who are last will be first.

For the kingdom of heaven is like a
landowner
who went out early in the morning
to hire men to work in his vineyard.
He agreed to pay them a denarius for the
day and sent them
into his vineyard.
About the third hour he went out and saw
others standing in the marketplace doing
nothing.
He told them,
"You also go and work in my vineyard,
and I will pay you whatever is right."
So they went.
He went out again about the sixth hour
and the ninth hour and did the same thing.
About the eleventh hour he went out and
found still others standing around.
He asked them,
"Why have you been standing here all day
long doing nothing?"
"Because no one has hired us," they
answered. He said to them, "You also go
and work in my vineyard."

When evening came,
the owner of the vineyard
said to his foreman,
"Call the workers and pay them their
wages, beginning with the last ones hired
and going on
to the first."

The workers who were hired about the
eleventh hour
came and each received a denarius.
So when those came who were hired
first, they expected to receive more.
But each one of them also received a
denarius.
When they received it, they began to
grumble
against the landowner.
"These men who were hired last worked
only one hour,"
they said, "and you have made them
equal to us who have
borne the burden of the work and the
heat of the day."
But he answered one of them,
"Friend,
I am not being unfair to you.
Didn't you agree to work for a denarius?
Take your pay and go.
I want to give the man
who was hired last the same
as I gave you.
Don't I have the right to do what I want
with
my own money?
Or are you envious because I am
generous?"

**So the last
will be first, and the first
will be last.**

23

The Two Sons

Matthew 21:28-32

What do you think?
There was a man who
had two sons.
He went to the first
and said, "Son, go and work
today in the vineyard."
"I will not," he answered,
but later he changed his
mind and went.
Then the father went
to the other son and said
the same thing.
He answered, "I will, sir,"
but he did not go.

Which of the two did what
his father wanted?
'The first," they answered.

Jesus said to them,
I tell you the truth,
the tax collectors and the
prostitutes are entering
the kingdom of God
ahead of you.

For John came to you
to show you the way
of righteousness,
and you did not believe him,
but the tax collectors
and the prostitutes did.
And even after you saw this,
you did not repent and
believe him.

The Tenants

Luke 20:9-18

He went on to tell the people this parable:
A man planted a vineyard,
rented it to some farmers and went away
for a long time.
At harvest time he sent a servant to the tenants so
they would give him some of the fruit of the vineyard.
But the tenants beat him and sent him away empty-
handed.
He sent another servant,
but that one also they beat and treated shamefully
and sent away empty-handed.
He sent still a third, and they wounded him and
threw him out.
Then the owner of the vineyard said, "What shall I
do?
I will send my son, whom I love;
perhaps they will respect him."
But when the tenants saw him, they talked the
matter over.
"This is the heir," they said.
"Let's kill him, and the inheritance will
be ours."
So they threw him out of the vineyard and killed him.

What then will the owner of the vineyard do to them?
He will come and kill those tenants and give the
vineyard to others.
When the people heard this, they said, "May this never be!"
Jesus looked directly at them and asked,

Then what is the meaning
of that which is written: "The stone
the builders rejected has become the capstone"?
Everyone who falls on that stone will be broken
to pieces, but he on whom it falls will be crushed.

The Wedding Banquet

Matthew 22:2-14

The kingdom of heaven is like a king
who prepared a wedding banquet for his son.
He sent his servants to those who had been invited
to the banquet to tell them to come,
but they refused to come.
Then he sent some more servants and said,
"Tell those who have been invited that I have
prepared my dinner:
My oxen and fattened cattle have been butchered,
and everything is ready. Come to the wedding
banquet."
But they paid no attention and went off—
one to his field, another to his business.
The rest seized his servants,
mistreated them and killed them.
The king was enraged. He sent his army
and destroyed those murderers and burned their
city.
Then he said to his servants,
"The wedding banquet is ready,
but those I invited did not deserve to come.
Go to the street corners and invite to the banquet
anyone you find."
So the servants went out
into the streets
and gathered all the people they could find, both
good and bad, and the wedding hall
was filled with guests.
But when the king came in
to see the guests,
he noticed a man there who was not
wearing wedding clothes.
"Friend," he asked, "how did you get in
here without wedding clothes?"
The man was speechless.
Then the king told the attendants, "Tie him hand
and foot, and throw him outside, into the darkness,
where there will be weeping and
gnashing of teeth."
For many are invited, but few are chosen.

The Fig Tree

Matthew 24:32-35

*Now learn this
lesson from the
fig tree:
As soon as its
twigs
get tender
and its leaves
come out,
you know that
summer
is near.
Even so, when
you see
all these
things, you
know that it is
near,
right at the
door.
I tell you the
truth, this
generation will
certainly not
pass away
until all these
things have
happened.*

**Heaven and
earth
will pass
away,
but my words
will never
pass away.**

The Faithful and the Wise Servant

Luke 12:41-48

Peter asked, "Lord, are you telling this parable
to us, or to everyone?" The Lord answered,
*Who then is the faithful
and wise manager, whom the master puts
in charge of his servants
to give them their food allowance
at the proper time?
It will be good for that servant
whom the master finds doing so
when he returns.
I tell you the truth, he will put him
in charge of all his possessions.
But suppose the servant
says to himself,
"My master is taking a long time in
coming," and he then begins to beat the
menservants and maidservants
and to eat and drink
and get drunk.
The master of that servant
will come on a day when he does not
expect him and at an hour he is not aware
of. He will cut him
to pieces and assign him a place
with the unbelievers.
That servant who knows
his master's will and does not get ready or
does not do what his master wants will be
beaten with many blows.
But the one who does not know
and does things deserving
punishment will be beaten with
few blows.*
**From everyone who
has been given much,
much will be demanded; and from the
one who has been entrusted with much,
much more will be asked.**

The Ten Virgins

Matthew 25:1-13

At that time the kingdom of heaven
will be like ten virgins who took their
lamps and went out to meet the
bridegroom.

Five of them were foolish
and five were wise.
The foolish ones took their lamps
but did not take any oil with them.
The wise, however, took oil
in jars along with their lamps.
The bridegroom was a long time
in coming, and they all became drowsy
and fell asleep.

At midnight the cry rang out:
"Here's the bridegroom!
Come out to meet him!"
Then all the virgins woke up and
trimmed their lamps.
The foolish ones said to the wise,
"Give us some of your oil; our lamps are
going out."
"No," they replied, "there may not be
enough for both us and you. Instead,
go to those who sell oil and buy
some for yourselves."
But while they were on their way
to buy the oil, the bridegroom arrived.
The virgins who were ready
went in with him to the
wedding banquet.
And the door was shut.
Later the others also came. "Sir! Sir!"
they said. "Open the door for us!"
But he replied, "I tell you the truth, I
don't know you."
**Therefore keep watch,
because you do not know the
day or the hour.**

The Talents

Matthew 25:14-30

Again, it will be like a man going on a journey,
who called his servants and entrusted his property to them.
To one he gave **five talents** of money, to another **two talents,** and to another **one talent**, each according to his ability. Then he went on his journey.
The man who had received the **five talents** went at once and put his money to work and gained five more.
So also, the one with the **two talents** gained two more.
But the man who had received the **one talent** went off, dug a hole in the ground and hid his master's money.
After a long time the master of those servants returned and settled accounts with them.
The man who had received the five talents brought the other five.
"Master," he said, "you entrusted me with five talents. See, I have gained five more."
His master replied, "Well done, good and faithful servant! You have been faithful with a few things;
I will put you in charge of many things. Come and share your master's happiness!"
The man with the two talents also came. "Master," he said, "you entrusted me with two talents; see, I have gained two more."
His master replied,
"Well done, good and faithful servant!
You have been faithful with a few things; I will put you in charge of many things.

Come and share your master's happiness!"
Then the man who had received the one talent came.
"Master," he said, "I knew that you are a hard man, harvesting where you have not sown and gathering where you have not scattered seed.
So I was afraid and went out and hid your talent in the ground.
See, here is what belongs to you."
His master replied, "You wicked, lazy servant! So you knew that I harvest where I have not sown and gather where I have not scattered seed?
Well then, you should have put my money on deposit with the bankers, so that when I returned I would have received it back with interest.
Take the talent from him and give it to the one who has the ten talents.
For everyone who has will be given more, and he will have an abundance.
Whoever does not have, even what he has will be taken from him.
And throw that worthless servant outside, into the darkness, where there will be weeping and gnashing of teeth."

The Sheep and the Goats

Matthew 25:31-46

When the Son of Man comes in his glory,
and all the angels with him, he will sit on his throne in heavenly glory.
All the nations will be gathered before him, and he will separate
the people one from another as a shepherd separates
the sheep from the goats.
He will put the sheep on his right and the goats on his left.
Then the King will say to those on his right,
"Come, you who are blessed by my Father; take your inheritance, the
kingdom prepared for you since the creation of the world.
For I was hungry and you gave me something to eat,
I was thirsty and you gave me something to drink,
I was a stranger and you invited me in,
I needed clothes and you clothed me,
I was sick and you looked after me,
I was in prison and you came to visit me."
Then the righteous will answer him,
"Lord, when did we see you hungry and feed you, or thirsty
and give you something to drink?
When did we see you a stranger and invite you in,
or needing clothes and clothe you?
When did we see you sick or in prison and go to visit you?"
**The King will reply, "I tell you the truth, whatever you did for
one of the least of these brothers of mine, you did for me."**
Then he will say to those on his left,
"Depart from me, you who are cursed, into the eternal fire
prepared for the devil and his angels.
For I was hungry and you gave me nothing to eat,
I was thirsty and you gave me nothing to drink,
I was a stranger and you did not invite me in,
I needed clothes and you did not clothe me,
I was sick and in prison and you did not look after me."
They also will answer,
"Lord, when did we see you hungry or thirsty
or a stranger or needing clothes or sick or in prison,
and did not help you?"
**He will reply, "I tell you the truth, whatever you did not do
for one of the least of these, you did not do for me."**

Then they will go away to eternal punishment,
but the righteous to eternal life.

The Growing Seed

Mark 4:26-29

He also said,
*This is what the kingdom of God is like.
A man scatters seed on the ground.
Night and day, whether he sleeps or gets up,
the seed sprouts and grows, though he does
not know how.
All by itself the soil produces grain—
first the stalk, then the head,
then the full kernel
in the head.
As soon as the grain is ripe, he puts the sickle to
it, because the harvest has come.*

The Watchful Servants

Luke 12:35-40

*Be dressed ready for service
and keep your lamps burning, like men waiting
for their master to return from a wedding banquet,
so that when he comes and knocks they can
immediately open the door for him.*

*It will be good for those servants whose master
finds them watching when he comes.
I tell you the truth, he will dress himself to serve,
will have them recline at the table and will come
and wait on them.*

*It will be good for those servants whose master
finds them ready, even if he comes
in the second or third watch of the night.
But understand this: If the owner of the house
had known at what hour the thief was coming, he
would not have let his house be broken into.*

**You also must be ready,
because the Son of Man will come at an hour
when you do not expect him.**

The Moneylender

Luke 7:36-43

Now one of the Pharisees
invited Jesus to have dinner with him,
so he went to the Pharisee's house and reclined at the table.
When a woman who had lived a sinful life in that town learned that Jesus
was eating at the Pharisee's house,
she brought an alabaster jar of perfume, and as she stood behind him
at his feet weeping,
she began to wet his feet with her tears.
Then she wiped them with her hair, kissed them and poured perfume on them.
When the Pharisee who had invited him saw this, he said to himself,
"If this man were a prophet, he would know who is touching him and what
kind of woman she is—that she is a sinner."
Jesus answered him,
Simon, I have something to tell you.
"Tell me, teacher," he said.
Two men owed money to a certain moneylender.
One owed him five hundred denarii, and the other fifty.
Neither of them had the money to pay him back, so he canceled the debts of
both.
Now which of them will love him more?
Simon replied,
"I suppose the one who had the bigger debt canceled."
You have judged correctly,
Jesus said.
Then he turned toward the woman and said to Simon,
Do you see this woman?
I came into your house.
You did not give me any water for my feet,
but she wet my feet with her tears and wiped them with her hair.
You did not give me a kiss, but this woman,
from the time I entered, has not stopped kissing my feet.
You did not put oil on my head, but she has poured perfume on my feet.
Therefore, I tell you, her many sins have been forgiven—for she loved much.
But he who has been forgiven little loves little.
Then Jesus said to her,
Your sins are forgiven.
The other guests began to say among themselves, "Who is this who even forgives
sins?"
Jesus said to the woman,
Your faith has saved you; go in peace.

The Good Samaritan

Luke 10:25-37

On one occasion an expert in the law stood up to test Jesus. "Teacher," he asked, "what must I do to inherit eternal life?"

What is written in the Law?
he replied.

How do you read it?
He answered:

"Love the Lord your God with all your heart and with all your soul and with all your strength and with all your mind"; and, "Love your neighbor as yourself."

You have answered correctly,
Jesus replied.

Do this and you will live.
But he wanted to justify himself, so he asked Jesus, "And who is my neighbor?"

In reply Jesus said:

A man was going down from Jerusalem to Jericho, when he fell into the hands of robbers. They stripped him of his clothes, beat him and went away, leaving him half dead. A priest happened to be going down the same road, and when he saw the man, he passed by on the other side.

So too, a Levite, when he came to the place and saw him, passed by on the other side. But a Samaritan, as he traveled, came where the man was; and when he saw him, he took pity on him. He went to him and bandaged his wounds, pouring on oil and wine. Then he put the man on his own donkey, took him to an inn and took care of him. The next day he took out two silver coins and gave them to the innkeeper. "Look after him," he said, "and when I return, I will reimburse you for any extra expense you may have." Which of these three do you think was a neighbor to the man who fell into the hands of robbers?

The expert in the law replied, "The one who had mercy on him." Jesus told him,

Go and do likewise.

The Friend in Need

Luke 11:5-13

Then he said to them,
*Suppose one of you has a friend,
and he goes to him at midnight and says,
"Friend,
lend me three loaves of bread,
because a friend of mine on a journey
has come to me, and I have nothing
to set before him."
Then the one inside answers,
"Don't bother me.
The door is already locked,
and my children are with me in bed.
I can't get up and give you anything."*

*I tell you, though he will not
get up and give him the bread because
he is his friend,
yet because of the man's boldness
he will get up
and give him as much as he needs.*

So I say to you:
**Ask and it will be given to you;
seek and you will find;
knock and the door will be opened to
you.**
*For everyone who asks receives; he who
seeks finds; and to him who knocks,
the door will be opened.
Which of you fathers, if your son asks
for a fish, will give him a snake instead?
Or if he asks for an egg,
will give him a scorpion?
If you then, though you are evil,
know how to give good gifts to your
children,
how much more
will your Father in heaven give
the Holy Spirit to those who ask him!*

The Rich Fool

Luke 12:13-23

Someone in the crowd said to him,
"Teacher, tell my brother to divide the
inheritance with me."
Jesus replied,
*Man, who appointed me a judge or an
arbiter between you?*
Then he said to them,
*Watch out! Be on your guard against all
kinds of greed;
a man's life does not consist in the
abundance of his possessions.*

And he told them this parable:
*The ground of a certain rich man produced a
good crop. He thought to himself,
"What shall I do?
I have no place to store my crops."
Then he said, "This is what I'll do.
I will tear down my barns and build bigger
ones, and there I will store all my grain
and my goods. And I'll say to myself,
'You have plenty of good things laid up for
many years. Take life easy; eat,
drink and be merry.' "
But God said to him,*
"You fool!
*This very night your life will be demanded
from you.
Then who will get what you have prepared
for yourself?"
This is how it will be with anyone who
stores up things for himself but is not rich
toward God.*

Then Jesus said to his disciples:
*Therefore I tell you, do not worry about your
life, what you will eat; or about your body,
what you will wear.*
**Life is more than food, and the body
more than clothes.**

The Unfruitful Fig Tree

Luke 13:6-9

Now there were some present
at that time who told Jesus about the
Galileans whose blood Pilate had mixed
with their sacrifices.
Jesus answered,
*Do you think that these Galileans
were worse sinners than all the other
Galileans because they suffered this
way?
I tell you, no!*
**But unless you repent,
you too will all perish.**
*Or those eighteen who died when
the tower in Siloam fell on them—do
you think they were more guilty than
all the others living in Jerusalem?
I tell you, no!*
**But unless you repent,
you too will all perish.**

Then he told this parable:
*A man had a fig tree,
planted in his vineyard, and he
went to look for fruit on it, but did not
find any.
So he said to the man who took care
of the vineyard, "For three years now
I've been coming to look for fruit on
this fig tree and haven't found any.
Cut it down! Why should it use up
the soil?"
"Sir,"
the man replied, "leave it alone for
one more year, and I'll dig around it
and fertilize it.
If it bears fruit next year,
fine!*
If not, then cut it down."

47

The Low Seat at the Feast

Luke 14:7-14

When he noticed how the guests
picked the places of honor at the table, he
told them this parable:

*When someone invites you
to a wedding feast,
do not take the place of honor,
for a person more distinguished than
you may have been invited.
If so, the host who invited both of you
will come and say to you,
"Give this man your seat."
Then, humiliated, you will have to take
the least important place.
But when you are invited, take the
lowest place, so that when your host
comes, he will say to you,
"Friend, move up to a better place."
Then you will be honored in the
presence of all your fellow guests.
For everyone who exalts himself
will be humbled, and he who humbles
himself will be exalted.*

*Then Jesus said to his host,
When you give a luncheon or dinner,
do not invite your friends, your brothers
or relatives, or your rich neighbors; if
you do, they may invite you back and
so you will be repaid.*
**But when you give a banquet,
invite the poor, the crippled,
the lame, the blind,
and you will be blessed.**

*Although they cannot repay you,
you will be repaid at the resurrection of
the righteous.*

The Great Banquet

Luke 14:15-24

When one of those at the table with him heard
this, he said to Jesus,
"Blessed is the man who will eat at the feast
in the kingdom of God."
Jesus replied:
*A certain man was preparing
a great banquet and invited many guests.
At the time of the banquet
he sent his servant to tell those who had
been invited,
"Come, for everything is now ready."
But they all alike began to make excuses.
The first said,
"I have just bought a field,
and I must go and see it. Please excuse
me."
Another said,
"I have just bought five yoke of oxen,
and I'm on my way to try them out.
Please excuse me."
Still another said, "I just got married,
so I can't come."
The servant came back and reported this
to his master.
Then the owner of the house became
angry and ordered his servant,
"Go out quickly into the streets and alleys
of the town
and bring in the poor, the crippled, the
blind and the lame."
"Sir," the servant said, "what you ordered
has been done, but there is still room."
Then the master told his servant,
"Go out to the roads and country lanes
and make them come in,
so that my house will be full.
I tell you, not one of those men who were
invited will get a taste
of my banquet."*

The Cost of Discipleship

Luke 14:25-35

Large crowds were traveling with Jesus,
and turning to them he said:
*If anyone comes to me and does not hate his
father and mother,
his wife and children, his brothers and sisters—
yes, even his own life—he cannot be my
disciple.
And anyone who does not carry his cross and
follow me cannot be my disciple.*

*Suppose one of you wants to build a tower.
Will he not first sit down and estimate the cost
to see if he has
enough money to complete it?
For if he lays the foundation and is
not able to finish it, everyone who sees it
will ridicule him, saying,
"This fellow began to build and was
not able to finish."*

*Or suppose a king is about to go to war
against another king.
Will he not first sit down and consider whether
he is able with ten thousand men to oppose the
one coming against him with twenty thousand?
If he is not able,
he will send a delegation while the other is still
a long way off and will ask for terms of peace.*

**In the same way,
any of you who does not give up everything
he has cannot be my disciple.**

*Salt is good, but if it loses its saltiness, how can
it be made salty again?
It is fit neither for the soil nor for the manure
pile; it is thrown out.
He who has ears to hear, let him hear.*

The Lost Coin

Luke 15:8-10

*Or suppose a
woman has ten
silver coins
and loses one.
Does she not
light a lamp,
sweep the house
and search
carefully
until she finds it?*

*And when she
finds it,
she calls her
friends and
neighbors
together
and says,*

*"Rejoice with me;
I have found my
lost coin."*

*In the
same way,
I tell you,*
**there is
rejoicing
in the presence
of the angels of
God over one
sinner who
repents.**

The Prodigal Son

Luke 15:11-32

Jesus continued:

There was a man who had two sons. The younger one said to his father, "Father, give me my share of the estate." So he divided his property between them. Not long after that, the younger son got together all he had, set off for a distant country and there squandered his wealth in wild living.

After he had spent everything, there was a severe famine in that whole country, and he began to be in need. So he went and hired himself out to a citizen of that country, who sent him to his fields to feed pigs. He longed to fill his stomach with the pods that the pigs were eating, but no one gave him anything.

When he came to his senses, he said, "How many of my father's hired men have food to spare, and here I am starving to death! I will set out and go back to my father and say to him: Father, I have sinned against heaven and against you. I am no longer worthy to be called your son; make me like one of your hired men."

So he got up and went to his father. But while he was still a long way off, his father saw him and was filled with compassion for him; **he ran to his son, threw his arms around him and kissed him.**

The son said to him, "Father, I have sinned against heaven and against you. I am no longer worthy to be called your son."

But the father said to his servants, "Quick!
Bring the best robe and put it on him.
Put a ring on his finger and sandals on his feet.
Bring the fattened calf and kill it.
Let's have a feast and celebrate.
For this son of mine was dead and is alive again; he was lost and is found."
So they began to celebrate.
Meanwhile,
the older son was in the field.
When he came near the house, he heard music and dancing.
So he called one of the servants and asked him what was going on.
"Your brother has come,"
he replied, "and your father has killed the fattened calf because he has him back safe and sound."
The older brother became angry and refused to go in.
So his father went out and pleaded with him.
But he answered his father, "Look!
All these years I've been slaving for you and never disobeyed your orders. Yet you never gave me even a young goat so I could celebrate with my friends.
But when this son of yours who has squandered your property with prostitutes comes home, you kill the fattened calf for him!"
"My son," the father said, "you are always with me, and everything I have is yours.
But we had to celebrate and be glad, because this brother of yours was dead and is alive again;
**he was lost
and is found."**

The Shrewd Manager

Luke 16:1-15

Jesus told his disciples:

There was a rich man whose manager was accused of wasting his possessions.
So he called him in and asked him, "What is this I hear about you?
Give an account of your management, because you cannot be manager any longer."
The manager said to himself, "What shall I do now?
My master is taking away my job.
I'm not strong enough to dig, and I'm ashamed to beg—
I know what I'll do so that,
when I lose my job here, people will welcome me into their houses."

So he called in each one of his master's debtors. He asked the first, "How much do you owe my master?" "Eight hundred gallons of olive oil," he replied.
The manager told him, "Take your bill, sit down quickly, and make it four hundred."
Then he asked the second, "And how much do you owe?"
"A thousand bushels of wheat," he replied. He told him,
"Take your bill and make it eight hundred."
The master commended the dishonest manager
because he had acted shrewdly.
For the people of this world are more shrewd in dealing with their
own kind than are the people of the light.

I tell you, use worldly wealth to gain friends for yourselves,
so that when it is gone, you will be welcomed into eternal dwellings.

Whoever can be trusted with very little can also be trusted with much,
and whoever is dishonest with very little will also be dishonest with much.
So if you have not been trustworthy in handling worldly wealth,
who will trust you with true riches?
And if you have not been trustworthy with someone else's property, who will give
you property of your own?
No servant can serve two masters. Either he will hate the one and love the other,
or he will be devoted to the one and despise the other.
You cannot serve both God and Money.
The Pharisees, who loved money, heard all this and were sneering at Jesus.
He said to them,
You are the ones who justify yourselves in the eyes of men,
but God knows your hearts.
**What is highly valued among men
is detestable in God's sight.**

The Rich Man and Lazarus

Luke 16:19-31

There was a rich man
who was dressed in purple
and fine linen and lived in luxury every day.
At his gate was laid a beggar named Lazarus, covered with sores
and longing to eat what fell from the rich man's table. Even the dogs
came and licked his sores.
The time came when the beggar died
and the angels carried him to Abraham's side.
The rich man also died and was buried.
In hell, where he was in torment,
he looked up and saw Abraham far away,
with Lazarus by his side.
So he called to him,
"Father Abraham, have pity on me and send Lazarus to dip the tip of
his finger in water and cool my tongue, because I am in agony in this
fire."
But Abraham replied, "Son, remember
that in your lifetime you received
your good things, while Lazarus
received bad things,
but now he is comforted here and you are in agony.
And besides all this,
between us and you a great chasm
has been fixed, so that those who want to go
from here to you cannot, nor can anyone cross
over from there to us."
He answered, "Then I beg you,
father, send Lazarus to my father's house,
for I have five brothers. Let him warn them, so
that they will not also come to this place
of torment."
Abraham replied, "They have Moses
and the Prophets; let them listen to them."
"No, father Abraham," he said, "but if someone from the dead goes to
them, they will repent."

He said to him,
**"If they do not listen to Moses and the Prophets,
they will not be convinced even if someone
rises from the dead."**

The Master and the Servant

Luke 17:5-10

The apostles said to the Lord,
"Increase our faith!" He replied,
*If you have faith as small as a
mustard seed,
you can say to this mulberry
tree,
"Be uprooted and planted in the
sea,"
and it will obey you.*

*Suppose one of you had
a servant plowing or looking after
the sheep.*

*Would he say to the servant
when he comes in
from the field,
"Come along now and sit down
to eat"?
Would he not rather say,
"Prepare my supper,
get yourself ready
and wait on me while I eat and
drink;
after that you may eat and
drink"?
Would he thank
the servant because he did what
he was told to do?*

*So you also,
when you have done everything
you were told to do, should say,*

**"We are unworthy servants;
we have only done
our duty."**

The Persistent Widow

Luke 18:1-8

Then Jesus told his disciples a
parable to show them that they
should always pray and not give up.
He said:
*In a certain town there was a
judge who neither feared God nor
cared about men.*

*And there was a widow in that
town who kept coming to him
with the plea,
"Grant me justice against my
adversary."
For some time he refused.
But finally he said to himself,
"Even though I don't fear God or
care about men,
yet because this widow
keeps bothering me,
I will see
that she gets justice,
so that she won't eventually
wear me out with her coming!"*

And the Lord said,
*Listen to what the
unjust judge says.
And will not God bring about
justice for his chosen ones,
who cry out to him day and
night?
Will he keep putting them off?
I tell you, he will see
that they get justice, and quickly.*

**However,
when the Son of Man comes,
will he find faith on the earth?**

The Pharisee and the Tax Collector

Luke 18:9-14

To some who were confident of their own righteousness and looked down on everybody else, Jesus told this parable:

Two men went up to the temple to pray,
one a Pharisee and the other a tax collector.
The Pharisee stood up and prayed about himself: "God, I thank you that I am not like other men—robbers, evildoers, adulterers—or even like this tax collector.
I fast twice a week and give a tenth of all I get."

But the tax collector stood at a distance. He would not even look up to heaven,
but beat his breast and said,
"God, have mercy on me, a sinner."

I tell you that this man, rather than the other, went home justified before God.

For everyone who exalts himself will be humbled, and he who humbles himself will be exalted.

Photos by: Page:
Pictor: Cover, 10–11, 14–15, 42–43, 46–47, 50–51, 62–63.
Tony Stone: 26–27, 30–31, 48–49, 56–57, 60–61, back cover.
Image Bank: 8–9, 18–19, 20–21, 28–29, 36–37.
Huber: 4–5, 12–13, 16–17, 22–23, 24–25, 32–33, 34–35, 38–39, 40–41, 52–53, 54–55, 58–59.
Silvestris: 6–7.
P. Östergrens: 44–45.